EVERYBODY WINS

The Chapman Guide to
Solving Conflicts Without Arguing

GARY D. CHAPMAN, Ph.D.

TYNDALE HOUSE PUBLISHERS, INC.
Carol Stream, Illinois

Visit Tyndale's exciting Web site at www.tyndale.com

TYNDALE and Tyndale's quill logo are registered trademarks of Tyndale House Publishers, Inc.

Everybody Wins: The Chapman Guide to Solving Conflicts without Arguing

Designed by Ron Kaufmann

Edited by Dave Lindstedt

Scripture quotations are taken from the *Holy Bible,* New International Version®. NIV®. Copyright © 1973, 1978, 1984 by International Bible Society. Used by permission of Zondervan. All rights reserved.

Library of Congress Cataloging-in-Publication Data

Chapman, Gary D., date.
  Everybody wins : the Chapman guide to solving conflicts without arguing / Gary D. Chapman.
    p. cm.
  Includes bibliographical references.
  ISBN-13: 978-1-4143-0014-6 (hc : alk. paper)
  ISBN-10: 1-4143-0014-X (hc : alk. paper)
  1. Marital conflict. 2. Conflict management. 3. Couples—Psychology.
4. Married people—Psychology. I. Title.
  HQ734.C465 2006
  646.7'8—dc22   2006021182

Printed in the United States of America

12   11   10   09   08   07   06
7   6   5   4   3   2   1

Table of Contents

Introduction

For more than thirty years, couples have been walking into my office seeking help. Almost without exception, they come in because of unresolved conflicts. They have argued for so long that each knows what the other is going to say. Their arguments have become predictable, but resolution eludes them. Exhausted, they have now come for professional help. However, I often sense that they view me more as a judge than a counselor, secretly hoping that I will pronounce their spouse guilty of illogical thinking and unreasonable demands.

Because I am a counselor and not a judge, I begin the arduous task of listening to their complaints. They review their well-worn speeches for me, certain that I will see the logic of their respective positions. I listen carefully and take notes, but as a counselor, I'm not as concerned with logic as I am about relationships. I know that in their hearts they want more than to resolve a disagreement. What they deeply long for is a better relationship. Behind the frustration of unresolved conflicts is the desire for harmony.

Loving relationships are fostered by understanding, not by winning arguments. So I begin to ask a question such as, "How do you feel when those words come out of his mouth?" or "What happens inside you when you hear her make that comment?" I listen, take notes, and ask more questions, seeking to discover the feelings that lie beneath the conflicts. No conflict will ever be resolved successfully unless we first understand the underlying feelings.

I also ask couples questions about values: "Why is this so important to you?" The answer to that question often reveals the values that created a conflict in the first place. If I don't understand their values, I will never comprehend why they feel so strongly about the issues. As a counselor, I am doing for these couples what they have never learned to do for themselves. I am seeking to understand them. Understanding fosters resolution and harmony.

When I did the research for my book *The Four Seasons of Marriage,* I encountered hundreds of couples who admitted to having a "winter" marriage; that is, their marriages were characterized by anger, disappointment, loneliness, negativity, discouragement, frustration, and hopelessness. Their relationships were detached, cold, harsh, and bitter. They felt alone and betrayed. They had hunkered down in the igloo and hoped for spring, but for many, spring never came.[†]

Almost all of these couples started their marriages in spring. They had great visions of a happy life together. They intended to make their spouse supremely happy. Life would be beautiful. But some of these couples went straight from spring to winter, skipping summer and fall altogether. Others could look back on a former season in their marriages when the flowers bloomed and the sun was shining. Now they have to admit that the flowers have been dead for a long time.

What brought these couples from the anticipation of spring to the harshness of winter in their marriage relationships? Almost without exception, the process involved unresolved conflicts. Differences emerged, and some of these differences became divisive. The couples had no training in how to resolve conflicts, so they ended up trying to convince their spouse of the validity of their own perspective by means of carefully worded arguments. When the arguments were unconvincing, they repeated them with more intensity

---

[†] The four seasons of marriage refer to the "climate" within a marriage relationship, not the "season of life" a couple is in or the literal season in which they were married. As I explain in the book *The Four Seasons of Marriage,* the natural seasons of the year provide us with an apt analogy for the changes that occur in a marriage relationship.

and blamed their spouse for being illogical and unreasonable. Eventually, tired of arguing, they withdrew from each other, and the coldness of winter settled over the marriage.

Couples have conflicts in all four seasons of marriage. Those who learn to resolve their conflicts spend more time in spring and summer. Those who fail to resolve conflicts inevitably drift to a fall or winter marriage. These unresolved conflicts create a sense of hopelessness for many couples. They see only two options: remain in the marriage and be miserable, or dissolve the marriage and hope that somewhere in the future they will find someone with whom they are "more compatible." Those who choose the latter option fail to realize that no marriage is without conflict.

I believe there is a third option: Couples who learn how to resolve their conflicts without arguing turn the coldness of winter to the hope and promise of spring. Whatever the season of your marriage—spring, summer, fall, or winter—I believe that your relationship will be strengthened if you can learn the art of resolving conflicts in a positive way.

In this short book, my objective is to help you learn how to understand your spouse so that you can resolve

conflicts rather than simply win (or lose) arguments. When you win an argument, your spouse is the loser. And we all know it's no fun to live with a loser. When you resolve a conflict, you and your spouse both win and your friendship is strengthened. Good marriages are based on friendship, not on winning arguments.

I wrote this book for the thousands of couples who will never seek the services of a professional counselor but who would desperately like to learn how to resolve conflicts. I have chosen to write in the language of everyday life, not with highly technical terminology or lofty theological concepts. My desire is that this book will enhance the quality of your marriage by teaching you how to resolve conflicts without arguing.

1

$\mathcal{L}$et's start at the beginning. In the dating phase of your relationship, chances are that you and your spouse were enamored with each other. You liked what you saw. You enjoyed spending time together. You could talk for hours. He or she was the most wonderful person you could imagine. In short, you were smitten. The courtship may have been long or short, but your positive feelings led you to the marriage altar, where you made a commitment "for better, for worse; for richer, for poorer; in sickness and in health; to love and to cherish, so long as we both shall live." The promises you made to each other were colossal, but at the time you fully intended to keep them. You were caught up in the current of love and it all seemed so effortless. You knew that you and your mate had differences, but you never thought that someday those differences would become divisive.

Unfortunately, the euphoric feelings of being in love have an average life span of two years.[1] Then we come back to the world of reality, where theoretical differences become actual. Some of these differences we come to view as assets. Alan likes to cook; Nancy doesn't. She likes to clear the table and wash dishes; he doesn't. These differences make for a harmonious mealtime experience. Alan and Nancy work together as a team, each using his or her expertise for the benefit of the other. They experience the pleasure of harmony and may even express it with statements such as, "We were meant for each other," "We are a perfect match," "Life could not be better," and "I'm so glad I married you." When differences are viewed as assets, and husbands and wives work together in harmony, life is beautiful.

Other differences may become divisive. Bob likes sports and spends every Monday night watching football. Jill says, "Football is fine for the players, who are making millions of dollars by bashing their bodies against one another, but why would people want to waste their lives watching other people play a stupid game?" Surely the man she married is smarter than that.

"It's just my way of relaxing," Bob says.

"It's just your way of wasting your life," Jill replies.

"You have got to be crazy. Every man in the world watches *Monday Night Football*."

"Only the losers."

"Look, I work five days a week. Give me a break and let me watch football on Monday nights."

"Sure you work. So do I. But how about *us*? Why can't we spend a night together? It's football, baseball, basketball, car races. And if nothing else is on, you watch that dumb wrestling. There's never any time for *us*." Jill starts to cry and walks out of the room. Bob turns off the TV and now the real fight begins. *Monday Night Football* gives way to a verbal boxing match. Before the evening is over, Bob and Jill will argue themselves into an intense state of unhappiness.

What did an evening of argument accomplish? Some might say, "Nothing," but that answer would be naive. The argument accomplished a great deal. For one thing, it created greater emotional distance between a husband and wife who now view each other as an enemy rather than a friend. Each feels the other is unreasonable and, perhaps, irrational. Not only that, but they have also stimulated feelings of hurt, anger, and resentment, and troubling questions are rushing to their minds:

"What has gotten into him?"

"What is her problem?"

"I can't believe the things she said."

"How could he be so cruel?"

"What happened to our love?"

"Have I married the wrong person?"

They may even end up sleeping in separate bedrooms that night, or lying stock still and rigid in the same bed as they silently replay the argument in their minds. Yes, the argument accomplished a great deal. Unfortunately, the accomplishments were all destructive.

Perhaps the only positive thing that came from the argument was that Bob and Jill identified a point of conflict in their marriage. He discovered that she intensely dislikes his watching *Monday Night Football,* and she discovered that he finds great pleasure in watching football on Monday nights. But because the argument did not resolve the conflict, it now stands as an emotional barrier between them that will affect the way they process their relationship. Now, every Monday night, Bob will watch television with a conscious awareness that he is displeasing his wife. And every Monday night, Jill will say to herself, "He loves football more than he loves me. What kind of husband is that?"

We'll come back to Bob and Jill later, but first let me clarify what I mean by the word *argue.* It is a word that is best known in the legal arena, where attorneys present arguments to show that a defendant is either guilty or not guilty. These arguments are statements made by the attorneys based on available evidence. They are designed to appeal to a jury's sense of logic and reason. The implication is clear: Any reasonable person would agree with my argument. On occasion, an attorney may also appeal to the emotions of a jury by presenting aspects of the case designed to stimulate empathy for the attorney's argument.

In a courtroom, arguments are perfectly permissible. In fact, cases could not be tried without arguments from both sides. Both attorneys present evidence and their interpretation of the evidence, seeking to convince the jury that their position is the correct one. Witnesses can be cross-examined, and implications can be challenged. The judicial system is based on the assumption that by means of argument and counterargument, we are likely to discover the truth about guilt or innocence.

We all know that the cause of justice is not always served in the courtroom, but at least the case is resolved. Defendants who are found not guilty go free. Defendants who are found guilty may pay a fine, be placed on probation, or go to prison, depending on the severity of the case. Or the case might be appealed to a higher court, in which case more arguments would be presented at each level of appeal until a final judgment is handed down. In every case, somebody wins and somebody loses. Occasionally, one might hear an attorney make a statement such as, "I thought our arguments were good, but apparently the jury was not convinced." Or the winning attorney might say, "We made our case. The arguments were solid, and I think the jury recognized the truth."

When you choose to argue with your spouse, you are electing to use a judicial system to convince your spouse of the truth or validity of your position. Unfortunately, what works fairly well in a court of law works very poorly in a marriage relationship, because there is no judge available to determine whether you or your spouse is "out of order." Arguments quickly become charged with emotion and you may end up yelling, screaming, or crying; pouring out words that assassinate your mate's character; questioning his or her motives; and condemning his or her behavior as unloving, unkind, and undisciplined.

When you argue, your objective is the same as it would be in a courtroom: You want to win the case. You want your side to be vindicated and your spouse to be found guilty of your accusations. This is what is so gravely harmful about arguments. They ultimately lead to one of three results: (1) You win and your spouse loses; (2) you lose and your spouse wins; or (3) you argue to a draw. When an argument ends in a draw, both spouses are losers. Neither one is convinced by the other's arguments, and both parties walk away disappointed, frustrated, hurt, angry, bitter, and often despairing of hope for their marriage.

None of these outcomes is good. The winner may feel good for a few moments or a few days, but eventually, living with the loser becomes unbearable. The loser walks away from an argument like a whipped dog that goes away to lick its wounds. It's not a pretty picture, but it's a common experience. In fact, it's so common that we have a saying for it: "He's in the doghouse." Being in the doghouse means that one spouse has incurred the displeasure of the other and must live at a distance until he or she can once again find the spouse's favor. When conflicts are not resolved and both spouses walk away with stinging words of rebuke and condemnation ringing in their ears, they will typically withdraw from each other emotionally and hope for a better day. If a better day does not come in time, they may eventually seek a "better partner" or resign themselves to the coldness of a winter marriage.

Any victory won by means of an argument will be short lived. The loser will eventually come back with a new argument (or an old argument restated) in an effort to persuade his or her spouse. But the renewed argument will also end with a win, lose, or draw verdict. So you see, arguments never resolve anything; they only reveal conflicts. Once a conflict is revealed, a couple must find a way to resolve it with dignity and with respect for the other person. I believe there are thousands of couples who would like to learn how to resolve conflicts without arguing. That is the purpose of this book.

PUTTING THE PRINCIPLES INTO PRACTICE

1. List three issues you and your spouse have argued about within the past year.

2. What do you find most painful about arguments?

3. What have arguments accomplished in your marriage?

4. On a scale of 1–10, how strongly are you motivated to find a better way to resolve conflicts?

2

*C*onflicts grow out of our uniqueness. Not only are males and females different, but each individual male and female is unique. Part of our uniqueness is genetically based. These genetic differences are most observable in our physical characteristics. No two fingerprints are exactly alike. Each person has unique facial characteristics. This is typically what allows us to recognize one another. Other differences are nonphysical. They sometimes fall into the category of what is commonly called personality differences. Though you can't observe these differences by simply looking at a person, they are just as real. When we use the words *introvert* and *extrovert,* we are describing a personality difference. Our differences also show in the way we perform the necessary tasks of daily life, such as loading a dishwasher, squeezing a tube of toothpaste, or hanging a roll of toilet paper. We have different ideas on how to raise children, how to drive a car, how to spend our leisure time, and a thousand other aspects of life. It is because of our differences that we experience conflicts, but I don't know anyone who would like to eradicate our differences and make us all clones.

The answer to conflict resolution is not in seeking to rid ourselves of our differences but in learning how to make our differences into assets rather than liabilities. The goal of a good marriage is for a couple to learn how to work together as a team, utilizing differences to make life better for both spouses. Resolving conflicts is one method by which we develop this teamwork. Sometimes, we don't even know what our differences are until a conflict arises.

When I use the word *conflict,* I'm not talking about simple disagreements such as her favorite

color is blue, his favorite color is yellow. That is not a conflict; it is simply a difference of opinion or preference. Conflicts are disagreements in which both spouses feel strongly and their differing opinions affect their behavior, causing disharmony in the relationship. Now, if the wife's preference for blue and the husband's preference for yellow is applied to painting the bathroom, their strongly held differences might erupt into a conflict in which they try to convince each other to paint the room a particular color. Conflicts can erupt in any area of life: driving, eating, money, sex, in-laws, spirituality, leisure time, and child rearing, to mention a few. Conflicts are not necessarily bad—and they're inevitable in every marriage. For one simple reason, it is impossible to be married and not have conflicts: You are married to a person and every person is unique. In marriage, our objective is not to get rid of conflicts, but rather to resolve conflicts and thereby learn how to work in harmony, as teammates, toward mutual objectives.

When I mentioned the conflict over what color to paint the bathroom, my mind flashed back to a young couple I counseled several years ago. Jerry and Iris had been married for two years and considered themselves to be in the spring season of their relationship; that is, until they decided to repaint their small apartment. They readily agreed upon the color for each room, until they came to the bathroom. He wanted blue and she wanted green. They were surprised to find themselves arguing passionately over something that they both realized was ultimately quite trivial. Yet they both felt so strongly about their opinions that, after a few rounds of argument, they agreed to go for counseling.

"We're actually ashamed to be here," Iris said. "This seems like such a trivial matter, but it has become very divisive in our marriage. And we don't want to end up fighting over what color to paint the bathroom."

With an apologetic shrug, Jerry said, "I bet you've never had a couple come to see you about what color to paint the bathroom."

I smiled and said, "Well, let's lay it on the table and look at it." Turning to Iris, I said, "I'm

sure you've told Jerry all the reasons why you would like the bathroom painted green. So, why don't you share those reasons with me?" She ran through her list and I took notes. When she was finished, I said, "That makes a lot of sense. I can understand why you would feel that way." She seemed relieved.

Next, I turned to Jerry and said, "I'm sure you have equally valid reasons why you would like the bathroom painted blue. So, why don't you share those with me?" When Jerry had shared his reasons, I repeated my response: "What you're saying makes a lot of sense. I can understand why you would like to have the bathroom painted blue." Jerry seemed relieved that I would agree with him, but Iris looked perplexed. She said, "But you agreed with both of us, and that doesn't solve our conflict."

"You are right," I responded. "But I don't think either of you is actually looking for a solution. You are still in the arguing mode and have not yet moved to the resolution mode."

"What do you mean?" Iris said.

"How did you feel when I affirmed your list of reasons for painting the bathroom green?" I asked.

"It felt good," she said. "It felt like you were respecting my ideas."

I looked at Jerry and asked, "How did you feel when I affirmed your ideas as making sense and told you I could understand why you would like to have the bathroom blue?"

"I felt like you were hearing me," he said, "like what I said made sense to you."

"What I did for each of you is what you have not yet done for each other," I said. "You have each argued your own position, but you have not affirmed the other person's ideas." I turned again to Jerry and asked, "Can you honestly say to Iris what I said to her? 'What you're saying makes a lot of sense. I can understand why you would want the bathroom painted green.' I think her ideas made a lot of sense. Do you agree?"

"Yes," he said, "but I like my ideas better."

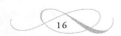

"That's understandable, but would you be willing to affirm her ideas by saying something similar to what I just said to her?"

"You mean now?"

"Yes, now would be a good time."

Jerry looked at Iris and said, "What you're saying makes sense to me. I can see why you would want the bathroom painted green. And besides that, I love you," he added with a smile. Both Iris and I smiled as well.

"Okay, that's a good start," I said. "And now, Iris, could you honestly make that statement to Jerry?"

She nodded at me and turned to face Jerry. "What you're saying also makes sense. And I can understand why you would want to have the bathroom painted blue. And I love you, too," she said.

"Now I think you are ready to look for a resolution," I said. "You are no longer enemies; you are two friends trying to solve a problem. So, what are the options?"

"We could paint it green," Jerry offered.

"Or, we could paint it blue," Iris said. "Or we could mix blue and green together and paint it aqua."

"I can think of another possibility," I added. "You could paint some walls blue and some walls green."

"I hadn't thought of that," Iris said.

"Neither had I," said Jerry.

"I've never seen a bathroom with two colors," said Iris.

"Neither have I," I interjected, "but it would be unique, wouldn't it? You would probably get lots of comments about it."

"I like that idea," Iris said. "What do you think, Jerry?"

"I think it's a great idea. We will have the most unique bathroom in the development. And when the neighbors ask us why the two colors, we can tell them about our conflict and how we resolved it."

"You might even save them a visit to a counselor," I said.

When a couple learn to resolve conflicts in this manner, when they work together to understand, encourage, and support each other, marriage becomes beautiful. The ancient Hebrew proverb "Two are better than one" becomes a reality.[1] Their deep, emotional need for companionship is met. They are connected with each other emotionally. They approach life with a sense of harmony and together will accomplish far more than either of them could accomplish alone.

On the flip side, unresolved conflicts become barriers to harmony. Life becomes a battlefield and husbands and wives become enemies. By means of verbal bombshells, they fight the same battles over and over again, inflicting injuries that push them even further apart emotionally. After an unrelenting series of unresolved conflicts, a husband might say, "We are just not compatible; we shouldn't have gotten married in the first place. We are like night and day. I don't see how we can ever get it together." His wife might respond, with tears flowing down her face, "How could it come to this when we enjoyed being with each other so much when we were dating? I don't understand where we went wrong." The academic answer to her question is simple: They never learned to resolve conflicts. Perhaps they never anticipated conflict. In the euphoria of the "in love" experience, couples seldom recognize differences and can hardly imagine serious disagreements.

The good news is that any couple can learn to resolve conflicts. I emphasize the word *learn*. The skill of conflict resolution does not come simply with the passing of time. As surely as you can learn to ride a bicycle, drive a car, or use a computer, you can learn how to resolve conflicts. It will require you to change some of your attitudes, learn to listen, treat your spouse with respect, and negotiate solutions, but it can be done. I'm not saying it will be easy, but the rewards for success are phenomenal.

Why is it so important to resolve conflicts? As one husband put it, "It's the difference between heaven and hell. For years, we were both miserable. But when we finally began learning how to resolve conflicts, I could see the light at the end of the tunnel. Now I know what it's like to be married and happy. I can't believe we waited so long to get help."

⁓

PUTTING THE PRINCIPLES INTO PRACTICE

1. What are some of the *differences* between you and your spouse that have caused conflicts?

2. In what way might these differences become assets if you learn to resolve conflicts and work as a team?

3. Conflicts that are resolved in a positive way create intimacy. Can you think of a recent conflict that you resolved in a positive way? What made the resolution positive? If a recent conflict wasn't resolved in a positive way, what kept you from reaching a resolution?

3

It's All about Attitude

*O*ften the difference between resolving conflicts and arguing is *attitude*. Why do people argue? In one word, *rigidity*. We adopt a rigid attitude and dig in our heels. In essence we're saying, "My way is the right way, and if you don't do it my way, then I will make your life miserable." This is the attitude of an *arguer,* a person who insists on getting his or her own way.

Conflict resolvers have a different attitude. They say, in effect, "I'm sure we can work this out in a way that will be positive for both of us. Let's think about it together." Spouses who adopt this attitude are looking for a win-win resolution.

Let's revisit Bob and Jill from chapter 1, who were arguing about *Monday Night Football*. Obviously, each of them saw the other's position as unreasonable. They created a miserable evening by arguing and were left with a huge barrier between them. But with a different attitude, the outcome could have been totally different.

What if Jill had chosen an attitude of accommodation? She might have said, "Bob, I know you really enjoy *Monday Night Football*. It's a way for you to unwind from the stresses of the day. On the other hand, I'm beginning to feel lonely and shut out of your life. That's not a feeling I want to have. So, at your convenience, I'd like for us to talk about it and look for a solution. I'm sure we can work it out. I love you very much, and I don't want this to come between us."

If Bob had chosen a conflict resolver's attitude, he might have responded, "Honey, you're right. I really do enjoy *Monday Night Football,* but I also value our relationship more than anything in the world. I want to meet your needs, and I'm sure we can find a solution that will be good for both of us. Why don't we talk about it at halftime?" The evening could have been pleasant for both Bob and Jill, and they likely would have found a solution that met their needs.

AN ATTITUDE OF RESPECT

Finding a winning solution begins by choosing to believe that such a solution is possible and that you and your spouse are smart enough to discover it. It begins when you recognize that you are married to another human being who is created in the image of God and is thus extremely valuable. It begins when you choose to treat your spouse as a person of worth. Starting with an attitude of respect predisposes that a couple will find a resolution to their conflict rather than put each other down with condemning arguments.

We recognize that all human beings are unique and that our differences do not diminish our worth. Thus, we choose to treat our spouses with dignity and respect. This means we will not seek to convince our spouses to be like us, to agree with all our opinions. We will give them the freedom to think and feel differently, and we will always respect their thoughts and feelings. When we choose an attitude of respect toward our spouses, we are less likely to allow ourselves to get caught up uttering condemning, harsh, cruel words.

Remember Jerry and Iris, who were having difficulty resolving their conflict about what color to paint the bathroom? What they discovered in the course of our counseling together was the calming effect of respecting each other's opinions. Both Jerry and Iris articulated their opinions very clearly, and they genuinely felt that their opinions were more valid than their spouse's. It was not until they expressed respect for each other's ideas that they moved from *attack mode* to *resolution mode*. As long as couples put down each other's ideas and judge them as less worthy, they are not likely to find a satisfactory resolution. But when they choose an attitude of respecting each other's ideas, even though they disagree with them, they create a climate in which they can look for a resolution *together*.

AN ATTITUDE OF LOVE

Another characteristic of conflict resolvers is that they choose an attitude of love. As one wife expressed it, "I am committed to my husband's well-being. I want to do everything I can to enrich his life and help him accomplish his objectives in life." If her husband has the same attitude toward her, then together they will find resolutions to their conflicts that will be beneficial to both of them. Selfishness is the opposite of love. Selfish people seek to impose their will on others. What is important to them is "getting my way." Lovers, on the other hand, seek to do those things that are most helpful for their spouses.

I saw an attitude of love graphically demonstrated when I visited John and Betsy. They had recently moved to our city and had visited our church. During our conversation, I discovered that they had lost a three-year-old son in a tragic boating accident a year earlier. They had two other children, who were now five and seven, and they told me that Betsy was now pregnant.

"Being a marriage counselor, Gary, I think you will find this interesting," Betsy said. "Our decision to have another child did not come easily. John really did not want another child, but I was strongly in favor of having another one."

I looked at John and he said, "The pain was so deep when we lost Josh that I couldn't bear the thought of going through that again. I was happy with the two children we had left and wanted to invest my time with them."

"I can understand that," I said.

Betsy continued, "I felt that my loss was so deep that I could never find healing without another baby. It was a real conflict between the two of us."

"So how did you resolve the issue?" I asked.

"We both respected each other's position," said John. "I knew that she really wanted to have another baby, and she knew that I didn't. And we knew that each of us was sincere."

"We prayed for God's wisdom," Betsy said. "One day while I was praying, God brought to my mind the story of Abraham offering his son Isaac on the altar to God. I knew that Abraham did that because of his deep love for God. Then a question came to my mind: 'Do I love John enough to offer my as-yet-unconceived child on the altar?' I've never loved anyone like I love John. He is a wonderful husband and father. I knew that my answer was yes. So I told John about my prayer and what God had brought to my mind, and I wanted him to know that I was willing to not have another child because I loved him so much."

"I cried like a baby when she told me that," John said. "Maybe it was the pent-up grief within me, but I sobbed uncontrollably for thirty minutes. I felt so overwhelmed by Betsy's love. I didn't say anything that night. I just cried and hugged Betsy. The next day, I went to work and reflected on what had happened. I was overcome by a deep sense of my love for Betsy, and I knew in my heart that I could never deprive her of having another child. I went home that night and told her that I wanted us to have another child. She was confused at first, because she knew how adamant I had been, but before the evening was over, she realized that my heart had sincerely changed and I wanted us to have another baby. So, as you can imagine," he said, "we're excited about the baby that is now inside Betsy's womb."

I nodded affirmingly as my eyes filled with tears. Finally, when I was able to speak, I said, "I don't know when I have ever seen such a deep demonstration of love. I think God has great plans for this child."

Love does not demand its own way but seeks the well-being of the one loved. It is an attitude of love that moves us toward resolving conflicts. The attitude of demanding our own way leads only to arguments.

AN ATTITUDE OF TOGETHERNESS

In the world of sports, success depends on teamwork. Whether in football, basketball, or auto racing, every team member has a job. When team members coordinate their efforts, they are more likely to meet their goals. Marriage is a team of two: a man and a woman. From a Christian perspective, the purpose of marriage is to process life together for the glory of God. Marriage is not about "me and my happiness." Marriage is about two people discovering and accomplishing God's plans for their lives.

A husband and wife bring an assortment of abilities to their marriage. When they see themselves as teammates, they realize that their game plan is not to compete against each other but to cooperate. It is this attitude of togetherness that creates a climate in which conflicts can be resolved. Conflicts are inevitable, but if a couple is committed to working together as a team, they can tackle the problem and not each other. An attitude of togetherness says, "We will not let this defeat us. We will find an answer."

Chuck and Rhonda had a major conflict over the behavior of their two-year-old son, Caleb. Chuck thought that the best way to discipline Caleb was to spank him. After all, that is what his own parents had done with him, and he had turned out all right.

Rhonda thought that spanking was barbaric. She never remembered being spanked by her parents. My first question was "Do you want Caleb to have two parents or one?"

"Well, two," said Chuck as Rhonda nodded affirmingly.

"Of course," I continued. "Do you want each of those two parents to do what is right in his or her own eyes, or do you want them to have the same game plan?"

"We've got to get on the same page," Chuck said. "What we've been doing is not working. It is destroying our marriage."

"It tears me apart when he spanks Caleb," Rhonda said.

"I don't want him to grow up to be irresponsible," Chuck said.

"I don't either," Rhonda replied.

"The two of you seem to have the same goal in mind," I observed. "You both want Caleb to grow

up to be a responsible young man." Chuck and Rhonda both nodded in agreement. "The conflict lies in the method of reaching that goal. Can we agree that you are teammates and not enemies?"

"Lately we've been acting like enemies," Rhonda said, "but I think both of us want to be teammates."

"It's fundamental that the two of you affirm that attitude," I said, "because if you continue to be enemies, Caleb will likely grow up to be irresponsible. Now, I'd like for you to hold hands and repeat after me . . ."

They both seemed a little shocked, but Chuck reached over and took Rhonda's hand.

"We are teammates," I said.

Chuck and Rhonda repeated, "We are teammates."

"Do you believe that?" I asked.

"Yes," they said in unison.

"Then let's get started."

I gave them a reading assignment for the following week. They were to explore how other couples feel about spanking and to discover what child-development experts have written on the subject. After Chuck and Rhonda did their research and we discussed their findings at some length, Chuck came to understand that there is more than one way to discipline a child, and Rhonda learned that spanking administered in the context of love is not as barbaric as she had assumed. Ultimately, they decided on three levels of response to Caleb's disobedient behavior: Level 1 was verbal reprimand; Level 2 was loss of privileges; Level 3 was spanking. They agreed to observe which type of discipline seemed to work best in changing Caleb's behavior. They also agreed that they would continue reading and would attend a parenting class for parents of preschoolers that was offered at their church. It was the attitude of togetherness that provided the foundation on which Chuck and Rhonda were able to build a positive plan of discipline for their son. Without this attitude, they might still have been arguing when Caleb was twelve.

In summary, it is an attitude of respect, love, and togetherness that leads to resolving conflicts. The good news is that we can—and do—choose our attitudes daily. Unfortunately, our default mode is selfishness, which leads us to proclaim, "My way is the right way." By nature, we are all self-centered, and that is why arguments are so common in marriage. However, with the help of God, we can choose an attitude of respect, love, and togetherness. Many of the couples I have worked with have found it helpful to put the following statements on an index card and post it in a prominent place in order to help them choose a winning attitude each day:

- I choose to respect my spouse's ideas, even when I disagree with them.

- I choose to love my spouse and do everything I can to help him or her today.

- I choose to believe that my spouse and I are teammates and that with God's help we can find solutions to our conflicts.

Choosing an attitude of respect, love, and togetherness leads us to listen carefully to one another. In the next chapter, we'll discuss how to listen empathetically.

～

PUTTING THE PRINCIPLES INTO PRACTICE

1. Memorize the following and use it with your spouse the next time you have a conflict: "I'm sure we can work this out in a way that will be positive for both of us. Let's talk about it. What are your ideas?"

2. Expressing respect for your spouse's ideas creates a positive atmosphere. Memorize the following statement and use it with your spouse the next time you have a conflict: "What you are saying makes sense to me. Now, let me share my thoughts and see if they make sense to you."

3. Selfish people seek to impose their ideas on others. Loving people seek to do what is best

for others. Rate yourself by placing an *X* on the line where it best indicates your attitude toward your spouse:

Selfish ———————————— Loving

4. Having an attitude of respect, love, and togetherness makes it possible to find win-win solutions to conflicts. How open are you to changing your attitudes?

4

*B*y its very nature, conflict reveals that two people have differing opinions and that they feel strongly about their own perspective. Along with every conflict comes a flag waving in the wind that reads, "Take time to listen." Conflicts cannot be resolved without empathetic listening. I use the word *empathetic* because most couples believe they are listening to each other, when in fact they are simply reloading their verbal guns. Empathetic listening means seeking to understand what the other person is thinking and feeling. It is putting ourselves in the other person's shoes and trying to look at the world through his or her eyes. It means that we have laid aside our verbal guns in favor of truly understanding the other person's point of view. Instead of focusing on how we are going to respond to what the other person is saying, we focus entirely on hearing what the other person is saying.

AFFIRM THE IMPORTANCE OF YOUR RELATIONSHIP

Empathetic listening begins when you affirm the importance of your marriage relationship. When conflicts arise, set the stage for resolution by carefully stating your objective: "I want to hear what you are saying because I know it is important to you and I value our relationship." I suggest that you write this sentence on an index card and read it out loud to yourself once a day until you memorize it, so that when a conflict arises, you will be ready to state your objective. Affirming the importance of your marriage relationship is a way of consciously choosing to put yourself in the role of *empathetic listener*—one who is seeking to discover your spouse's thoughts and feelings. If you don't consciously remind yourself that you are a listener, then you will likely revert to being an arguer.

I remember David, who said to me, "Your comment about choosing to be a listener was the most helpful thing for me. I went home and made myself a sign out of construction paper that read, "I AM A LISTENER." Whenever JoAnne and I have a conflict, I put the sign around my neck to remind myself of what I'm doing. My wife always smiles and says, 'I hope it's true.' The sign helps me remember to listen before I speak." By use of this simple device, David trained himself to be an empathetic listener.

Most people will need some training to become good listeners, because we are *responders* by nature. One research project found that the average person listens for only seventeen seconds before interrupting to give their own opinion. Such quick responses are what trigger arguments.

Natalie and Hunter had been married for fifteen years when they came to me for counseling. Natalie was on the verge of leaving the relationship.

When I asked about the nature of the problem, she responded, "He never listens to me. All we ever do is argue. Nothing ever gets settled. I'm sick of arguing."

When I turned to Hunter, he said, "We don't argue all the time. We have some good times—in fact, more good times than bad times. It's just that when she gets upset about something, she wants me to agree with her. But I don't always agree with her, and so we argue. I don't think we argue any more than other couples."

"I don't care about other couples!" Natalie said, "I care about *us*. You don't even know who I am, because you don't listen long enough to find out. You are always right. You don't ever have time to hear my opinions. How could you possibly disagree with them?"

As I glanced back at Hunter, he said, "This must be more serious than I realized."

"What did you hear Natalie saying?" I asked.

"I heard her saying that I don't know who she is. And maybe she's right."

"Would you like to know who she is?" I inquired.

"I don't know," he said. "I might hear some things I don't want to hear."

"But if they are true," I probed, "would you rather hear them or would you rather have Natalie clam up in silence and never share with you what she's thinking and feeling?"

"I'd rather hear them," he said.

"Then why don't we use the next ten minutes as a listening session. You and I will listen to Natalie as she describes for us how she views your relationship. Neither of us will respond to anything she says. We will simply try to understand what is going on in her mind. You may not like what she says, and you may not agree with what she says, but for the moment, we're simply trying to find out what she's thinking and what she's feeling. I may ask her a question or two to stimulate her thinking, but I don't want you to say anything, Hunter. I want you just to listen."

For the next ten minutes, Hunter listened while Natalie spoke. It was the first of many "listening sessions" we were to have over the next three months. Through this process, Hunter took the first step in resolving their conflicts.

In the beginning stages of learning to listen, couples often find it helpful to establish a specific amount of time for each spouse to be the listener. Once they have developed the art of listening, they can remove the artificial time restraints, and the listening sessions will become more conversational. But they shouldn't jump the gun; first they must learn to listen.

CLARIFY WHAT YOU HEAR YOUR SPOUSE SAYING

The second step in empathetic listening is to clarify what you hear your spouse saying. This is the classic technique of "active listening," in which you simply repeat to your spouse what you think he or she has said, without judging it to be good or bad. David, the husband who wore the "I am a listener" sign, said to his wife, JoAnne, "What I hear you saying is that you feel disappointed because I don't take the garbage out every day without your asking. I hear you saying that you wish I would take that responsibility seriously and that when you have to remind me, it makes you feel like you're my mother. And you don't want to be my mother; you want to be my lover. Actually, you didn't say that last part, but I get the feeling that's what you are saying. Is that right?"

JoAnne responded, "Yes, you're right. I do want to be your lover, and it's difficult when I have to remind you every day to do such a simple chore. I've got so much to do, especially since the baby came. That's just one thing I wish I didn't have to worry about."

David said, "I hear you saying that you feel overworked since the baby came. And if I would consistently take out the garbage without your asking, it would lighten your load."

"That's right," JoAnne said. "It's a little thing, but it means a lot to me."

"I can understand that," David said, "and I can

do that. What time of the day would you like me to take it out?"

"Right after dinner each evening," JoAnne said, "before you get involved in other activities. If you wait till morning, it becomes smelly, and I don't like to start my day with a full trash can."

"Okay, I'll do it," David said. "I didn't realize it was that important to you."

"I've been telling you for months," JoAnne said.

"I know you have," David said, "but I guess I never listened. The next time you get upset with me, remind me to put on my listening sign so that I can really hear what you're saying."

David used clarifying questions to make sure he understood what JoAnne desired. Without asking these questions, he might never have known what his wife was truly thinking and feeling. He also learned why she had this desire and how it affected her emotions toward him. Once he clearly understood her thoughts and feelings, he was able to make an intelligent, considerate response. Taking the trash out on a daily basis without being asked was a small price to pay to enhance his marriage relationship. If David hadn't used these clarifying questions, he and JoAnne might have entered into an extended argument over the pros and cons of who should take out the garbage. The argument would have left them estranged, hurt, and resentful. Instead, empathetic listening brought their conflict to a healthy resolution.

GIVE YOUR SPOUSE YOUR UNDIVIDED ATTENTION

The third aspect of empathetic listening is that you give your spouse your undivided attention. Don't try to watch television, read a magazine, or drink a Pepsi while listening to your spouse. One of the purposes of empathetic listening is to make sure that your spouse knows that he or she has been heard. When you lay everything else aside and give your spouse your undivided attention, you communicate that your relationship is more important to you than anything else. Without saying a word, you tell your spouse that you want to know what he or she is thinking and feeling. Focused attention is even more effective if you make eye contact with your spouse, nod your head affirmingly at appropriate moments, refuse to fiddle with a pencil or look out the window, and—whatever you do—don't walk out of the room while your spouse is talking.

If you're like some people, giving your spouse your undivided attention will be extremely difficult. I remember a woman who said to me, "I only have a couple of hours after dinner, after the children are in bed. I have a thousand things to do. If my husband has a problem, he wants me to sit down and listen to him. I tell him I can listen to him while folding the clothes. No, he wants me to look at him while I'm listening. Come to think of it, why doesn't *he* fold the clothes while I'm giving the baby a bath? Then maybe I could give him my full attention." For this wife, the sheer volume of household work made it difficult for her to give her husband her undivided attention.

On the other hand, many men pride themselves on being able to do three things at once. As one husband said, "I'm wired for multitasking. I can't imagine doing only one thing. When my wife insists that I sit down and listen to her, I feel like I'm in a straitjacket, like I'm wasting time. I could easily be listening to her while reading the report that I need to give the next day. It makes her furious when I try to do that. But I can honestly hear everything she's saying and read my report at the same time." This husband is being totally honest, but he exhibits little understanding of the dynamics of human relationships.

Here's what undivided attention communicates: "You are the most important person in my life. I want to hear what you are thinking and feeling because I value our relationship."

— vs —

On the other hand, here's what listening while doing something else communicates: "You are one of my many interests. Please continue to talk; I'm listening." Distracted listeners are often surprised when their spouse stops talking, walks out of the room, goes to the bedroom, and starts crying. Empathetic listening requires that you give your spouse your undivided attention.

SHARE YOUR OWN IDEAS ONLY WHEN YOUR SPOUSE FEELS UNDERSTOOD

The fourth characteristic of empathetic listening is that you never share your own perspective until your spouse has assured you that he or she feels understood. The most common mistake couples make in communication is responding before they have the full picture. This inevitably leads to arguments. Listen for as long as your spouse has something to say. Use clarifying questions to make sure you understand what he or she is thinking and feeling. When your spouse assures you that he or she feels that you understand, then it is time to give your own perspective. Often, determining this right time is best done with a series of questions:

"Do you feel that I understand what you are saying?" If your spouse says no, then let him or her continue explaining.

"Do you think I understand how you feel?" Again, if not, then let your spouse explain more fully.

When the answer to both questions is yes, then

you can ask, "Can I tell you what I'm thinking and feeling?" If your spouse says yes, then you can proceed to share your perspective. Your spouse now becomes the listener.

The fact that your spouse now feels heard and understood makes it easier to shift from the arguing mode to the listening mode. Now your spouse can honestly say to you, "I'm ready to hear you because I feel as if you understand my concerns. I know that you have a perspective that is equally as valid as mine, and I want to hear it." Your spouse now gives you his or her undivided attention, repeating what you say and asking clarifying questions until you feel heard and understood.

Empathetic listening creates a positive emotional climate. Arguing creates a negative emotional climate. Conflicts are resolved more easily when the climate is friendly rather than adversarial.

Had David failed to practice empathetic listening when JoAnne first mentioned her concerns about the garbage, he might have said, "Okay, I'll take the garbage out. Don't bring it up again." The conversation would have been over, but the conflict would not have been resolved. It was because he fully heard her perspective before he responded that they were able to resolve their conflict easily. When people respond too quickly, they often respond to the wrong issue. They need to listen long enough—and ask enough clarifying questions—to discover what is really at the heart of their spouse's complaints.

Many times, the real conflict is not about football or which color to paint the bathroom walls but about personality differences or unmet emotional needs. For example, people with a controlling personality will feel emotionally unsettled if things are not done in a timely manner and with some degree of perfection. On the other hand, people with low self-esteem may feel condemned if their spouse expresses strong expectations. Feeling condemned may lead either to "fighting back," trying to prove their worth, or to withdrawing in silent suffering.

Empathetic listening allows us to hear what is going on beyond or underneath the words that are being said. Through empathetic listening, we seek to understand the feelings that lie behind the words and to discover why the other person feels so strongly about the issue. Understanding creates an emotional climate where conflicts can be resolved.

When Natalie told Hunter, "You don't know who I am," she finally got his attention. After Hunter learned the skills of empathetic listening, he said to me, "This has been the most insightful experience of my life. No one ever taught me how to listen. Why didn't I have a class on this in college? It could have saved me fifteen years of arguing. I can't believe how much pain I've put Natalie through over these years by not listening to her. I had come to believe that arguing was just part of life. I assumed that all couples argued as much as we did. It's amazing how close I feel to her now. I really feel like I know her. And what's more important, *she* feels like I know her." Hunter had learned the awesome power of empathetic listening.

Most of us have had little experience in empathetic listening. Thus, it will take effort and time to change argumentative patterns of communication. Empathetic listening requires a change of mind-set.

It is a conscious choice to hear your spouse clearly. You create an atmosphere for empathetic listening when you say to your spouse, "I want to hear what you are saying because I know it is important to you and I value our relationship." Having stated your objective, give your spouse your undivided attention. Put the book down, turn the TV off, and lay aside the pencil. When your spouse stops talking, repeat what you have heard him or her say, making clarifying statements such as, "What I hear you saying is . . ." or "I think what you said is . . ." "Is that right?" Continue to ask clarifying questions until your spouse assures you that he or she feels heard and understood. Although this approach to listening may be difficult to learn, it is extremely rewarding because it will lead you and your spouse to greater understanding.

PUTTING THE PRINCIPLES INTO PRACTICE

1. Memorize this statement and use it with your spouse the next time you have a conversation

or a conflict: "I want to hear what you are saying because I know it is important to you and I value our relationship."

2. Consider making a sign that reads: "I am a listener." Pick it up and hold it while your spouse is talking.

3. Try this response the next time your spouse shares an idea: "What I hear you saying is _____. Is that correct?"

4. When your spouse starts talking, put down the magazine or turn off the television, and give your spouse your undivided attention. Look into his or her eyes as you listen.

5. Do not share your own perspective until you get a positive response to these three questions:

    "Do you feel as if I understand what you are saying?"

    "Do you feel as if I respect your ideas?"

    "Is this a good time for me to share my thoughts?"

6. After each conversation, using the scale of
   1–10, rate yourself on how well you followed
   suggestions 1–5 above.

5

LISTENING LEADS TO UNDERSTANDING

*J*ulie and Brian were arguing about going to see her parents.

"We were just down there two weeks ago," Brian said.

"I know," said Julie, "but Sunday is my mother's birthday."

"Then send her a card," said Brian.

"I don't believe you!" said Julie. "You are the most selfish person I have ever met."

"Well then, you haven't met very many people,"

GARY CHAPMAN

Brian replied. "I don't know any man who wants to visit his in-laws every two weeks."

"I'm not asking you to go every two weeks," Julie said as she started sobbing and walked out of the room.

Brian and Julie have never learned how to listen empathetically. But now let's imagine that they had read chapter 4 and were trying to be empathetic listeners. The conversation might have gone like this:

"Why do you want to go to your parents again this weekend? We were just there two weeks ago."

"I know, but this Sunday is my mother's birthday."

"Are birthdays a big deal in your family?"

"Yes, they are. My sister and I have given Mom a birthday dinner every year since we were five years old. I still remember that first year, when Dad helped us make cupcakes and decorate them."

"So your sister is going to be there on Saturday?"

"Oh, yes, she wouldn't miss it."

"Is her husband also coming?"

"Unless he has to work. Some years, he has to work and can't get away."

"Do you want me to go with you? Or would you rather go by yourself?"

"I want you to go with me, Brian. It's a family thing and I want you to be a part of it."

"Okay, on a scale of 1–10, how strongly do you want me to go?"

"Ten."

"Okay, then I'll go."

"Oh, Brian, I love you so much."

Why did things turn out so differently in the second scenario? Because Brian listened empathetically before he responded. His listening led him to understand how important the birthday party was to Julie and how strongly she wanted him to participate.

On the other hand, Brian also has opinions. He wants his relationship with Julie to be authentic, so he says to her, "Would you like to know why I was hesitant at first about going to your parents' this Saturday?"

"I assume it was because we were just there two weeks ago."

"That's part of it, but there's more to it than that. Would you like to hear it?" (Brian is trying to help Julie get into the listening mode.)

"Yes," Julie says as she sits down on the couch and looks at him.

"I was invited to play on the all-star team of the church softball league. I was really excited about it—you know how much I love to play softball—but when I realized how important this was to you, I felt that being with you was more important than playing softball."

"Oh, Brian, now I love you even more. I can't believe you are willing to give up the all-star team in order to be with my family."

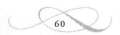

After a moment of reflection, Julie asks, "What time is the softball game?"

"Two o'clock. Why do you ask?"

"It just occurred to me that maybe you could play in the game and come to Mother's later. Dinner isn't until six. You might be a little late, but that would be all right. On a scale of 1–10," Julie says with a smile, "how strongly do you feel about playing in the game?"

"Do you really want to know?"

"Certainly," Julie says, still smiling.

"About a nine."

"Then, let's do it that way. I don't mind at all if you get there a little late."

"But that would mean driving two cars," Brian says. "And we wouldn't be together driving down and back."

"We'll make up for it when we get home."

"You're serious, aren't you?"

"Yes, I am."

"Julie, you are incredible. I love you so much."

In this scenario, it was Julie's efforts to listen empathetically that led her to understand how important the softball game was to Brian. Both Brian and Julie displayed an attitude of respect, love, and togetherness, which brought them to a win-win resolution of their conflict.

Many couples argue about conflicts rather than resolving them because they never come to understand each other's point of view. They spend their energy promoting their own perspectives rather than seeking to understand their spouse's perspective. Understanding involves the following four objectives, all of which can be obtained by empathetic listening:

1. *Know what your spouse is really saying.* This is not as easy as it sounds. In fact, one of the most common mistakes that couples make is responding to what they *think* their spouse is saying, without actually *listening* to what is

being said. For example, Brian's initial interpretation was that Julie wanted to visit her
parents a couple of times a month. This
misunderstanding stimulated negative
emotions inside of him. However, he had
not yet heard what Julie was actually saying.
She was talking about a birthday dinner, a
long tradition, and family values. Had Brian
listened empathetically, he would have heard
and understood what was really important
to Julie.

2. *"Hear" your spouse's feelings.* In his initial
encounter with Julie, had Brian been listening, he would have heard his wife expressing
the emotions of hurt, disappointment, and
anger. But because he was not listening
empathetically, Brian did not hear these
emotions. His failure to listen left Julie
sobbing and the conflict unresolved.

3. *Discover what is truly important to your
spouse—and why.* Had Brian listened empathetically, he would have discovered why
it was so important to Julie to go to her

mother's birthday dinner. It was a long-standing tradition, accompanied by warm feelings of family togetherness. Brian would have discovered that Julie's desire for him to be with her at this celebration hinged on the value she placed on family gatherings. Conversely, had Julie listened empathetically to Brian, she would have discovered why playing in the softball tournament was so important to him. It was an honor to be selected and had strong ties with his sense of self-esteem and his commitment to the team.

4. *Determine how strongly your spouse feels about his or her perspective.* Using a 1–10 scale is an easy way to determine how strongly your spouse feels about an issue. In fact, this is often the easiest place to begin when you are trying to understand your spouse. If you and your spouse are discussing Christmas shopping, for example, you might ask, "On a scale of 1–10, how strongly do you feel about my going shopping with you?" If your spouse responds with a number between 7 and 10

and your own desire is between 1 and 4, then you know that you must quickly shift into listening mode if you are going to resolve this conflict.

You might then ask, "When would you like to go shopping? How long would you like me to shop with you? What would you like my role to be in the process?"

These questions are designed to determine what your spouse truly desires. Then you might ask, "How would you feel if I decided not to go shopping with you?" or "How would you feel if I decided to go shopping with you?" The answers to these questions will reveal not only your spouse's feelings but also what impact your decision will have on your relationship.

Next, you can ask, "Why is my going shopping with you so important?" You may discover that the reason your spouse values your participation is that he or she sees it as a measure of the health of your marriage. Perhaps your spouse's parents always did their Christmas shopping together and it was an event that communicated, "We enjoy being together." On the other hand, you might discover that the reason it is so important to your spouse is that he or she feels very ill-prepared to select gifts for your parents and really needs your input. There may be any number of reasons why your spouse considers your participation so important. It is by means of empathetic listening that you will discover not only what your spouse is saying but also how he or she is feeling and why this issue is so important.

The sense of being understood and affirmed by one's spouse is a major step in creating an atmosphere where conflicts can be resolved. "I hear what you are saying, and it makes a lot of sense to me" is a million-dollar statement in resolving conflicts. It is what everyone longs to hear in conflict situations. We all want to be understood and affirmed.

Empathetic listening is the exact opposite of the argument approach, in which both parties are more interested in asserting their own opinions than in taking time to understand what the other is saying, thinking, and feeling. Asserting one's own opinion without first listening comes across as rejection and condemnation, which foster defensive feelings and resentment. That is why arguments lead to emotional distance. Empathetic listening, on the other hand, leads to understanding and affirmation.

Couples are not likely to resolve conflicts in a positive way if they do not understand each other. Understanding comes from listening and asking clarifying questions. When husbands and wives understand what their spouses are saying, why an issue is so important to them, how strongly they feel about it, and the emotions that accompany their desires, only then can they have intelligent and loving responses. Spouses who love each other by taking time to understand each other will be able to resolve conflicts in a healthy way.

PUTTING THE PRINCIPLES INTO PRACTICE

1. Many couples argue about conflicts rather than resolve them because they never come to understand each other's point of view. Here are four questions to help you understand your spouse:

- What is my spouse saying?

- What is my spouse feeling?

- Why is this important to my spouse?

- On a scale of 1–10, how strongly does my spouse desire this?

2. Once you understand your spouse, you have an opportunity to give an intelligent and loving response. How intelligent and how loving was your response in your most recent conflict with your spouse?

6

*T*hroughout this book, we have indicated that conflicts are inevitable. There are no marriages without conflicts. However, conflicts need not be divisive. If you choose a "win-win attitude" and you sincerely listen to your spouse, you will come to understand what he or she is thinking, feeling, and desiring. You will also discover why your spouse has these opinions and how strong these opinions are. With this information, you are now in a position to resolve conflicts in a positive manner. You are ready to ask the question, "How can we resolve this conflict so that both of us will feel loved and appreciated?" The answer to this question will lead to positive resolutions. By asking this question, you are not demanding your own way and you are not seeking to manipulate your spouse into agreeing with you—you are seeking to find a resolution that will make both you and your spouse feel good.

A husband and wife who understand and love each other can focus on finding a mutually agreeable solution rather than condemning each other. They are friends, not enemies. Together they will find a positive solution.

Typically, resolutions fall into one of three categories: meeting in the middle, meeting on one side, or meeting later.

MEETING IN THE MIDDLE

In this approach, the couple finds a solution approximately halfway between each of their original desires. Both spouses give up some of what they want, but both also gain some of what they want. Some people have called this approach "reaching a compromise." However, a compromise focuses on what both parties have given up. I prefer to focus on what they have gained. "Meeting in the middle" communicates to me that both parties have agreed on a solution that they feel is mutually loving and beneficial.

I met John and Brenda in Mobile, Alabama. They approached me after a seminar, and John said very excitedly, "This is our second time to attend your seminar. We attended last year when you were in Montgomery, and today we brought six couples from our church. We found it so helpful that we wanted to expose them to your teaching."

"Give me a specific example of how you found the seminar helpful," I said. Here is the story they shared with me:

John and Brenda knew that their old car, which had 215,000 miles on it, would soon need to be replaced. John wanted to buy a new car, and Brenda wanted to buy a used one. They realized they had a conflict over the issue one night when John came home and said, "I stopped by the Buick place today and priced some new cars."

"Why did you do that?" Brenda said. "We can't afford a new car."

"New cars are not much more expensive than used cars," John said. "Besides, they are much more reliable."

"Not if we get a late-model used car that has a warranty," said Brenda.

"I don't want to buy somebody else's junk," said John.

"I'm not talking about junk. I'm talking about finding a good, low-mileage used car," said Brenda.

With each exchange of words, the volume of their responses increased. When John realized that they were screaming at each other, he said, "I do believe that we have a conflict. I seem to remember hearing something about conflict resolution in that seminar we attended last month. Maybe we need to pull out our notes and see what was said."

"Better yet," Brenda said, "I've just finished reading the book *The Four Seasons of Marriage*.

There's a chapter in there on empathetic listening. I remember thinking as I read it, *That's a chapter we need to discuss with each other.*"

"I don't want us to get into a conflict over whether we should read the chapter or look at the notes," John said, smiling. "So why don't you review the chapter and I'll review the notes, and tomorrow night we'll share what we have learned about conflict resolution. I'm sure we're not the only ones who have wrestled with this topic, and I certainly don't think either one of us wants to get into a fight over this."

"Good idea," Brenda said. "But I don't want us to get ourselves in debt and do something we can't afford to do."

"I think we both agree on that," said John. "Obviously we don't agree on the question of new car vs. used car. But as smart as we are, I'm sure we can figure it out." He reached out and gave Brenda a hug.

"Okay," I said. "I can't wait to hear how you resolved the conflict."

Brenda spoke first. "Well, first we shared with each other some of the key ideas we had learned about how to listen. Then we tried to apply them to our situation. After we listened to each other, I realized that John had always wanted to have a new car. He had driven used cars all his life and had a number of experiences where he missed appointments and was inconvenienced by car troubles."

"And I learned," John said, "that Brenda was genuinely concerned about our finances. I didn't realize that she was living under so much pressure. That was one of the good things that came out of our listening to each other. Growing up, her dad had always bought reliable used cars, and she never remembered a car breaking down. I guess my experience was with older used cars that weren't very reliable."

"So how did you finally resolve the conflict?" I asked.

"After a lot of listening," John said, "and checking several options, we decided not to buy a car at all."

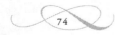

I'm sure John saw the puzzled look on my face, because he smiled as he continued, "We decided to lease a new car for three years."

"The monthly payments were just about the same," said Brenda, "and it was a payment that we both felt we could live with."

John continued, "At the end of three years, we hope to be in a better financial position, and then we can revisit the issue of buying a new car or a used car."

John and Brenda illustrate a positive approach to resolving conflicts by "meeting in the middle." John got to drive a new car and Brenda got a monthly payment that she felt they could afford. Both ended up feeling good about the resolution, and both felt loved and affirmed by the other. Many conflicts can be resolved by this "meeting in the middle" approach to conflict resolution.

MEETING ON ONE SIDE

This approach involves the same process of empathetic listening and affirming each other's ideas and feelings as meeting in the middle. But the final resolution is made by one spouse choosing to meet the other on the other spouse's side.

Betty and Mark illustrate this approach to conflict resolution. They came to my office because they had been arguing for three months over Betty's desire to go back and finish her undergraduate college degree. She had dropped out of college after her junior year when she and Mark got married. They had moved across country at the request of his employer. Now, nine years later, they were back in their hometown. Mark had a good job, and they had two children, the youngest of whom had just started first grade. Betty now felt that this was an ideal time for her to go back and finish her degree. Mark felt strongly that for Betty to go back to school would be a waste of time, energy, and money. "I'm making all the money we need," he said. "She doesn't need to go back and get her degree. She doesn't really want to work, anyway, so what's the purpose in getting a degree? The kids need help with their homework, and I don't really have time to do that. It's going to put a lot of pressure on our family."

"He doesn't understand how important it is for me to finish my degree," Betty said. "All my brothers and sisters finished college, and I'm the only one who doesn't have a degree. It will take only a year, and I can still help the children with their homework. Besides, Mark could help if he were willing to give up a little TV."

It was obvious to me that Betty and Mark not only had a conflict but also had spent considerable time arguing and were now at the point of throwing barbs at each other. It took a number of counseling sessions to help them come to respect each other's desires and to treat each other with dignity and love. Eventually, they learned to listen to each other empathetically. Mark was finally able to say, "I understand why it is so important for Betty to get her degree. I guess I was looking only at the financial side and the impact it would have on our family. I was not looking at her emotional need to finish her degree. I realize that I was self-centered and not willing to sacrifice in order to help her reach that goal. I have decided to support her enthusiastically in getting her degree. We've turned it into a family project. The kids are excited about it, and I realize now that this is going to have a positive effect on them. I hope that seeing Betty go back to finish her degree will motivate them to want to graduate from college themselves someday."

"How does this make you feel, Betty?" I asked.

"I feel very loved and affirmed by Mark," she said. "I'm sorry it took us so long to get here, but I think that he genuinely understands my desire. I really appreciate his love and support. I think it's going to make our marriage much stronger."

Mark and Betty's conflict was resolved by his choice to "meet on one side"—in this case, hers. The process of empathetic listening led them to understanding, and understanding led to a resolution they both agreed on. The conflict was no longer a barrier; it was genuinely resolved by Mark's choice to meet Betty on her side. Many conflicts can be resolved by this positive approach.

MEETING LATER

A third approach to resolving conflict is "meeting later." In this approach, a couple cannot honestly

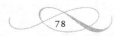

find a place to meet in the middle, nor can one spouse conscientiously move to the other side. Therefore, they "agree to disagree" with respect and love. This approach may resolve a conflict temporarily or permanently, depending on the nature of the disagreement. First, I'll illustrate how this approach works as a temporary resolution.

It is almost midnight on a Tuesday. Brad and Renee have been arguing for the past two and a half hours about whether he should go fishing at the end of the month with a group of guys from work. Brad really wants to go. He feels it is important for building rapport with his coworkers and that it would be good for him in terms of job security and possible promotion. Renee is resisting the idea because her perception is that most of Brad's coworkers are not the kind of guys he should be hanging out with. "Half of them are unfaithful to their wives," she says, "and almost all of them drink in excess. I just don't think it's a healthy climate."

It's well past their usual bedtime and both of them are fatigued. Their arguments have gotten them nowhere, and they now have a decision to make. Either they can continue to argue through the night and both face the new day emotionally and physically drained, or they can call a truce, acknowledging that the conflict is not resolved but that both of them need a break. In short, they can agree to disagree—temporarily. In essence, they are saying to each other, "We know this conflict is not resolved, but because it's late and we're both tired, we're going to put it on the shelf and agree that we will pick it up again tomorrow or at some other agreed-upon time. In the meantime, we will both give thought to how we might approach the issue in a more constructive manner, and we agree not to throw any more bombs at each other." They have agreed to a truce, and they both know that the truce is temporary.

If Brad and Renee do not learn to listen empathetically and seek to understand each other before they sit down to talk again, their next session may be as frustrating and unproductive as the last, and resolution may still elude them. However, if they do learn how to listen empathetically and understand each other's desires, they might create a much warmer atmosphere in their relationship. Through empathetic listening, they will learn to appreciate each other's point of view, even if they still honestly disagree. Instead of arguing, they'll now be able to express respect and love for each other. Renee may not be able to bring herself to meet Brad on his side, and Brad may be equally unable to meet Renee on her side, but they can still communicate amicably with each other. This means they will not treat each other harshly or allow distance to come between them. They will go on with life in a positive way, realizing that they simply have a conflict that is not yet resolved.

Sooner or later, of course (before the end of the month), they must move to a solution. If they fail to "meet in the middle" or "meet on one side," the day for the fishing trip will arrive and Brad will either go or stay at home. If he stays at home with resentment toward Renee, it will show up in his behavior and the unresolved conflict will have a detrimental effect on their relationship. If he goes on the fishing trip without regard to Renee's thoughts and feelings, her hurt and anger will be revealed by her behavior and the relationship will be damaged. Therefore, in this illustration, the decision to "meet later" is only a temporary solution that requires additional empathetic listening and understanding.

In other cases, the decision to "meet later," or to "agree to disagree," can be a permanent resolution of the conflict. For example, Nina and Tyler have a conflict over toothpaste. She is a middle squeezer and he squeezes from the bottom. For the first year of their marriage, they exchanged friendly but frank objections to the way the other squeezed the tube. Eventually, they got around to talking about it with some level of openness. They both agreed that, from an engineer's perspective, squeezing from the bottom made more sense. But from the perspective of Nina's sanguine personality, always squeezing from the bottom was a discipline that seemed impossible for her to learn. Neither Nina nor Tyler seemed able to consistently squeeze the way the other desired. Instead, they agreed to buy two tubes of toothpaste and let both of them squeeze the way they pleased. This solution will work for a lifetime—or until they discover the pump! They agreed to disagree, and neither held any animosity toward the other. They were simply no longer irritated by the other's behavior. They found a mutually satisfactory solution in choosing to agree to disagree.

Many of the common conflicts experienced in the early years of marriage can be resolved by "agreeing to disagree." I remember that when Karolyn and I were first married, we argued numerous times over how to properly load the dishwasher. I contended (and still do) that if you place like things together—plates with plates, cups with cups, and so on—they will come out cleaner and be less likely to get broken in the dishwasher. Karolyn argued that such organization was a waste of time. Dishwashers are designed to wash whatever is in them, no matter how or where the dishes are placed. After many months of arguing, we were left with anger and resentment.

When we finally learned to listen empathetically and sought to understand each other rather than seeking to win the argument, we ultimately agreed to disagree. The practical solution was that when Karolyn loaded the dishwasher, she could load it her way, and when I loaded the dishwasher, I would load it my way. Because I was the one who unloaded the dishwasher each morning, I agreed to clean the spoons that had been cradled together with peanut butter between them and to occasionally toss a broken glass into the trash. It was a small price to pay for marital harmony, and this solution has served us well for more than forty years.

Most conflicts can be resolved by "meeting in the middle," "meeting on one side," or "meeting later." Conflict resolution is much easier when we feel understood and loved and when we have reached the decision without coercion. We realize that we are on the same team and are working together to use our ideas, desires, and emotions to reach win-win solutions to our conflicts.

Each of these three patterns of conflict resolution requires empathetic listening, understanding, loving attitudes, and an openness to change. The reason that many couples do not resolve conflicts is that they never learn to follow the process of listening, understanding, and loving. They are stuck in a pattern of selfishly demanding their own way.

But listening, understanding, and loving is what creates a climate for mutually satisfying conflict resolution.

PUTTING THE PRINCIPLES INTO PRACTICE

1. Memorize this question and use it with your spouse next time you have a conflict: "How can we resolve this conflict so that both of us will feel loved and appreciated?"

2. In this chapter, we discussed three positive ways of resolving conflicts:

    - "Meeting in the middle"

    - "Meeting on one side"

    - "Meeting later"

    Did you use any of these strategies in resolving a recent conflict? Did you and your spouse both feel loved and appreciated?

3. Can you think of an illustration where "meeting later" or "agreeing to disagree"

became a permanent solution to one of your conflicts?

4. In your opinion, how well are you and your spouse doing in reaching win-win solutions? What do you need to change, or continue, in order to improve?

7

$\mathcal{A}$t the beginning of a seminar in Chattanooga, Tennessee, my associate Rick Pierce asked couples who had been married for forty years or longer to raise their hands. Several hands were raised. He then narrowed the field to those who had been married for at least forty-five years, and then fifty. When Rick said, "Okay, fifty years or longer," only one couple's hands were still raised.

"So, how long have you folks been married?" Rick asked.

"Fifty-two years." I made a mental note to talk to this couple during the lunch break.

When I met up with James and Mildred, I asked, "To what do you attribute your long marriage?"

James replied, "We made a commitment early in our marriage that whenever we had a disagreement, we would listen to each other and try to find a solution that we both thought was right. As you can imagine, we had a lot of differences, especially in the early years. We spent a lot of time listening and looking for solutions. But it all paid off because we've lived in harmony for fifty-two years. We have four children, all of whom are happily married. Mildred and I could not have asked for a better life."

I turned to Mildred and asked, "Would you like to add anything to that?"

"Well, I think he's right," she said. "The only thing I would add is that we made a commitment also to love each other, no matter what happened, and to be there for each other. I came down with multiple sclerosis a few years ago. Physically, things have gotten worse for me, but James has been there for me through the whole time. I could not have asked for more support."

"And what brought you to my seminar?" I asked.

"For years, we've made it a practice to attend a marriage enrichment weekend every year," Mildred replied.

"We read your book on the five love languages a few years ago," James added, "and we decided that if you ever came to Chattanooga, we would come to hear you."

"I'm glad you came," I said. "I hope you will find it helpful." As I turned to walk away, I added, "I wish every couple in the country could hear what you have just told me. If every couple made the commitment to listen to each other and resolve their differences, to be supportive of each other no matter what happens, and to continue growing by attending marriage enrichment events and reading books on marriage, we would see a radical change in the marriages of this generation."

James responded with a laugh and said, "Feel free to put our comments in your next book, and maybe the whole world will hear it."

"Maybe I'll do that," I said. And so I have.

I am always thrilled to meet couples like James and Mildred, who have learned how to resolve conflicts and walk together in harmony over a lifetime. On the other hand, I have been deeply pained by the many couples whom I have observed arguing with each other, verbally berating each other, and destroying their dream of what marriage should be.

James and Mildred epitomize the mind-set that leads to conflict resolution rather than arguing. First, they were committed to resolve conflicts, and to do so in a way that respected both spouses' ideas. Every unresolved conflict stands as a barrier to marital harmony. Every resolved conflict brings a deeper sense of intimacy. The decision to seek resolution is a decision to build marital harmony.

Second, they built harmony in their marriage by committing to love each other no matter what happened and to be there for each other. Many couples do not understand that love is a choice and not a feeling. It is a decision to look out for the best interests of their spouse. It begins with an *attitude* and expresses itself in *behavior* that seeks to make life easier for the other person. It is a willingness to *give* so that they can *build up* the life of their spouse. Couples who fail to understand that love is an attitude rather than a feeling may never find marital unity. If we simply follow our feelings, we will treat each other kindly when we have positive feelings, and we will treat each other harshly when we have negative feelings. Husbands and wives who allow their emotions to control their behavior will forever be arguing. On the other hand, those who choose an attitude of love and seek to implement it on a daily basis will create a climate where conflicts can be resolved in a way that respects the opinions and feelings of both spouses.

The third bit of wisdom that James and Mildred shared was the understanding that marriage is perpetually in process. We must continue to grow and learn throughout the years. The fact that James and Mildred attended my seminar after fifty-two years of marriage indicates that their mind-set was one of continual learning. Mildred said, "For years, we've made it a practice to attend a marriage enrichment weekend every year." And James told me that they regularly read books on marriage as a couple.

There are many ways of stimulating marital growth. Marriage enrichment weekends and books about marriage were the two that James and Mildred shared. A couple might go for marital counseling, watch a recorded marriage enrichment seminar on VHS or DVD, or listen to such a program on CD. Many churches also offer marriage enrichment classes that meet weekly or monthly. Many couples have found these to be extremely informative and supportive.

Couples who build their marriage on this three-part foundation—the decision to seek reconciliation, the commitment to love and support each other no matter what, and the dedication to continually involve themselves in activities that stimulate marital growth—will succeed in resolving conflicts without arguing.

I've never met a couple who enjoyed arguing, but I have met thousands of couples who argue regularly. Arguing is based on the unspoken assumption that "my way is the best way." Arguing seeks to prove that the spouse's ideas are inferior. Arguing stimulates negative emotions. Arguing communicates condemnation and strikes at the other person's self-esteem. To sum it up, arguing creates disunity between husbands and wives.

Arguments, by their very nature, create an atmosphere of antagonism. Couples quickly become adversaries rather than friends. I have never known a couple who argued themselves into harmony, but I have worked with many couples who have argued themselves into hopelessness.

Marital conflicts are inevitable, but arguing is an option—an unhealthy option. Arguments never resolve conflicts; they simply intensify them. Unresolved conflicts over a period of months or years have led many couples to the conclusion that they are not compatible. In their minds, if they were, they wouldn't have so many conflicts and would be able to resolve them easily. But the truth is that every couple has conflicts, and conflict resolution is not easy. Because we are all egocentric, we believe that any sane and mature person would agree with our opinions. Conversely, anyone who disagrees with us needs to be educated—so we set about educating our spouses. But they too have an egocentric worldview, and they are trying to educate us. The result is argument and disunity.

In this book, I have sought to point to a higher road. Marital conflicts can be resolved, but it requires that we get off our stallions of superiority and view each other as human beings who are uniquely crafted in God's image. Because we are all individuals, our thoughts, feelings, and desires will be different from one another's. However, along with our individuality comes a deep need for intimacy. Marriage is designed to meet that need. A husband and wife come together with their differences to form a team where each will use his or her strengths to help the other, and together they will use their abilities to make the world a better place to live. Each of us is uniquely crafted by God with certain interests and abilities to accomplish positive purposes when we cooperate with God and with each other. In a healthy marriage, the partners work together as a team to help each other accomplish the objectives and goals that each believes he or she is destined to fulfill. When the team works together in harmony, marriage becomes all that it was designed to be.

Conflicts give us an opportunity to demonstrate our love, respect, and admiration for each other. When we accept conflicts as a normal part of marital team dynamics, we will create time to listen to each other. We will learn how to listen effectively so that we understand our spouse's thoughts, desires, and feelings. And together, we will find solutions that allow us to work together as a team, supporting each other rather than allowing our differences to divide us.

Conflict resolution is one of the most fundamental aspects of marital success. The bottom line is that unresolved conflicts, accompanied by arguing, destroy marriages. Conflicts that are resolved by listening to each other, respecting each other, and negotiating solutions will strengthen our marriages. It is my desire that you will learn how to resolve your marital conflicts without arguing.

PUTTING THE PRINCIPLES INTO PRACTICE

1. James, who had been married fifty-two years, said, "We made a commitment early in our marriage that whenever we had a disagreement, we would listen to each other and try to find a solution that we both thought was right." Have you and your spouse made a similar commitment? If not, why not?

2. Mildred said, "We made a commitment also to love each other no matter what happened, and to be there for each other." Have you and your spouse made a similar commitment? If not, why not?

3. James and Mildred made it a practice to attend a marriage enrichment weekend every year and to read books on marriage. Have you and your spouse made a similar commitment? If not, why not?

4. If your spouse will not join you in making these commitments, don't despair. You can

have a positive influence on your spouse by learning and practicing the techniques in this book. In fact, your most powerful influence will be your example. As you change your approach from "arguer" to "solution seeker," you will enhance the emotional climate in your marriage.

EPILOGUE

*T*he ideas I have shared in this book were not devised in an ivory tower. They grow out of thirty years of listening to couples who have spent hours arguing and have come to the point of desperation. They come from more than forty years of experience in my own marriage. What I have shared with couples in counseling, I have now shared with you. But I am fully aware that knowledge alone is not enough. In order to be helpful, knowledge must be applied to life. Now that you have read the book, I want to challenge you to read it again, this time with your spouse. (You've already seen that the chapters are short, so you know we're not talking about a great deal of time.) Share your answers to the questions at the end of each chapter. Your answers will reveal your thoughts, feelings, and desires related to the topic of the chapter. Then, as conflicts arise in your marriage, seek to apply the principles you have read and discussed with each other.

Argumentative patterns from the past will not die quickly, but you can learn a better way. It will take time and effort, but it is effort well invested. If the two of you can learn to resolve your conflicts without arguing, you will experience the joy of working in harmony as a team. This is what marriage is all about: a husband and wife using their unique ideas, emotions, and desires to strengthen each other's lives. Resolving conflicts in a healthy manner deepens a marriage relationship. You can learn to resolve conflicts without arguing.

If you find this book helpful, I hope you will share it with a friend. If you have stories to share with me, I invite you to select the Contact link at www.garychapman.org.

- When you win an argument, your spouse is the loser. And we all know it's no fun to live with a loser.

- Arguments accomplish a great deal. Unfortunately, the accomplishments are all destructive.

- As surely as you can learn to ride a bicycle, drive a car, or use a computer, you can learn how to resolve conflicts.

- The answer to conflict resolution is not in seeking to rid ourselves of our differences but in learning how to make our differences into assets rather than liabilities.

❧ Finding a winning solution begins by choosing to believe that such a solution is possible and that you and your spouse are smart enough to discover it.

❧ Arguments never resolve conflicts; they simply intensify them.

❧ Three winning attitudes:

1. I choose to respect my spouse's ideas, even when I disagree with them.

2. I choose to love my spouse and do everything I can to help him or her today.

3. I choose to believe that my spouse and I are teammates and that with God's help we can find solutions to our conflicts.

❧ Conflicts cannot be resolved without empathetic listening. I use the word *empathetic* because most couples believe they are listening to each other, when in fact they are simply reloading their verbal guns.

🔊 Empathetic listening requires that you give your spouse your undivided attention.

🔊 The most common mistake couples make in communication is responding before they have the full picture. This inevitably leads to arguments. . . . When people respond too quickly, they often respond to the wrong issue.

A RESOLUTION BY WHICH EVERYBODY WINS

WHEREAS: arguing creates an adversarial relationship; and

WHEREAS: resolving conflicts is absolutely essential if we are to work together as a team:

THEREFORE, BE IT RESOLVED: That we shall commit ourselves to seek win-win solutions to our conflicts

By learning to listen empathetically:

What is my spouse saying?

What is my spouse feeling?

By choosing to respect each other's ideas and feelings,

By seeking to understand why a particular issue or point of view is so important to my spouse, and

By finding solutions that leave both of us feeling loved and appreciated.

Ratified, this _____ day of _____, 2____.

_____
HUSBAND

_____
WIFE

⌐ *Notes*

CHAPTER 1
1. Dorothy Tennov, *Love and Limerence* (New York: Stein and Day, 1979), 142.

CHAPTER 2
1. Ecclesiastes 4:9.

About the Author

Dr. Gary Chapman is the author of the perennial best seller *The Five Love Languages* (more than 3.5 million copies sold) and numerous other marriage and family books. He is currently working with best-selling author Catherine Palmer on a new fiction series based on *The Four Seasons of Marriage,* the first book of which is scheduled to release in the spring of 2007. Dr. Chapman is the director of Marriage and Family Life Consultants, Inc.; an internationally known speaker; and the host of *A Growing Marriage,* a syndicated radio program heard on more than 100 stations across North America. He and his wife, Karolyn, live in North Carolina.

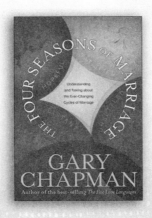

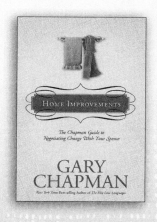

CONFLICT IS INEVITABLE.
ARGUING IS A CHOICE.

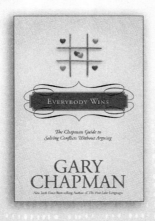

Relationship expert Dr. Gary Chapman provides a simple blueprint to help you and your spouse find win-win solutions to the everyday disagreements that crop up in every marriage. Solving conflict without arguing will leave you and your spouse feeling loved, listened to, and appreciated.